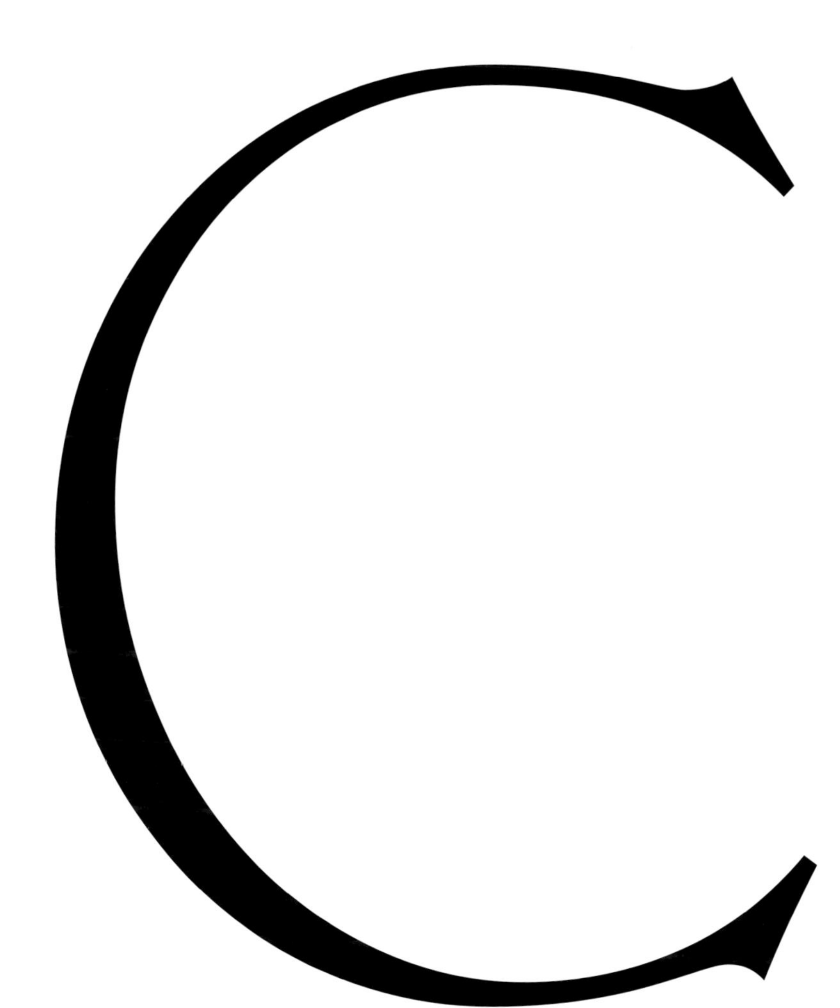

CRYSTALS

HAT & BEARD | LOS ANGELES   DILETTANTEPAPER

CONTENTS

SACRED SCIENCE: EXPLORING THE LIFE OF CRYSTALS

"Crystals are living beings at the beginning of creation."

—Nikola Tesla

Forged by fire and fluid, and the slow, heavy press of the earth's surface, crystals are nature at its most miraculous, science as it veers into the mystical.

We've been drawn to them since the birth of man, from Stone Age totems hewn of granite to Egyptian amulets carved of vivid lapis lazuli. There are the jade idols of the ancient Orient, the marble Gods of the Greeks, Native American turquoise talismans, the crystal ball whispering its secrets to Gypsy wagon seers.

Born of billions of years of force and pressure, intense fluctuations in temperature, and the orderly convergence of interlocking atoms, crystals are mathematic and cosmic, logical and divine. Shaped by both symmetry and chaos, their form is cleanly dictated by a tidy arrangement of atoms, but their varied hues are the result of eloquent imperfection.

It is the faults, the unexpected impurities within a crystal's structure that births their prismatic array of colors—the delicate violet of amethyst, the blood rich red of garnet, the iridescent glow of moonstone.

At their most flawless, they appear liquid, jagged shards of clear water held captive in the air. Believing quartz to be ice so cold it could never thaw, the ancient Greeks gave them their name, "Krystallos."

In a way, crystals are alive. Like us, they start microscopic and evolve, atoms furiously combining to add weight, substance, texture, shape. Subterranean, secretive, they branch out, stretching, pushing far into the dark. They move, mesh, and grow. If no space is left, they simply join together, bind, bond, and unify.

Like the endless symmetry of snowflakes, the combination of crystal forms is nearly infinite. The repeated pattern, nature's doubling and tripling (and on and on) of itself, propels the crystal always forward, layer upon layer upon layer.

In 1900, the physicist Nikola Tesla wrote, "In a crystal we have a pure evidence of the existence of a formative life principle, and although in spite of everything we cannot understand the life of crystals, it is still a living being."

For centuries, we have been granting crystals inherent meaning and influence, believing them to be imbued with protective, healing and shamanic powers. We worship them, we adorn ourselves with them, we offer them up to our gods.

This book showcases specific properties that have been assigned, over hundreds of years of study, to particular stones. Philosophers, scientists, scholars, and mystics each have had their own intimate relationship to crystals, their own interpretations of their use.

Aside from the shaman, it is the scientist who has been most intensely seduced. We are immersed today in a modern technology that owes much of its evolution to the study of crystals and the ability to harness their inherent properties.

Radios, clocks, sonar, cigarette lighters, automobiles and satellites would not exist without the incorporation of crystal science and the unique ability of quartz to receive, process and transmit energy in precise vibrational patterns.

These attributes have had an effect on our civilization that is nothing short of miraculous. Crystals enable us to transmit, amplify, and store various frequencies of energy, including sound, electricity and, perhaps most astoundingly, information. The computer chip evolved from this very concept, a tiny grain of silicon quartz the key building block to a technology that has ultimately revolutionized our entire reality.

Crystals now act as the lodestone, the beating heart, the breath, of every digital device on our planet.

This book is a culmination of research, shared knowledge and discussion. It was created as a simple guide, a way of deepening our relationship to crystals, and in a larger sense, to the natural world around us.

A fascination with crystals is a fascination with science, the earth, the planets, the cosmos. Whether you subscribe to a specific religious or spiritual belief system or adhere to a pragmatic atheism, crystals are transfixing.

They are exquisitely flawed, intimidatingly perfect, deeply mysterious. They are nature in her most compelling form, a breathtaking example of elements—air, fire, earth, water—combining into one.

Crystals are born both in the globe's fiery core and in the frozen reaches of space. They are dug up from black dirt or arrive blazing from the sky, bits of star stone, tossed down from above.

And what could be more magical than that?

But belief is not required. Only the ability to be awed—by nature, by physics, by geometry, by science.

And if you want magic, it's here too.

Our Advisors

As stated in our introduction, this book is a culmination of research, shared knowledge and discussion.

We could not have created this publication without the incredible wisdom and guidance of our key advisors, Mark Phillips and Martin Anguiano of the Los Angeles crystal shop, Spellbound Sky.

Both veterans of the fashion industry, Mark and Martin shared a vibrant history as designers in the apparel business, working independently and as a design duo for numerous high profile labels.

Transcendental interest has always played a big role in both of their lives, and eventually crystals and stones evolved into a mutual obsession that inspired them to leave the fashion world and take that leap of faith toward creating a world that reflected their true spiritual passion.

Much gratitude goes to both these gentlemen for being so kind, patient, and insightful and for so generously sharing their extensive knowledge of crystals and crystal healing.

We highly recommend exploring the wonderful Spellbound Sky shop and surrounding community—Mark and Martin are truly inspirational.

—Jessica Hundley
  Los Angeles, California, 2017

CLEANSING CRYSTALS

There are numerous methods of cleansing crystals, varying from the practical to the metaphysical. Some prefer to utilize ancient, ritualistic methods to cleanse negative energies from crystals that have been newly purchased or are regularly handled. Others simply want their crystals gleaming, clean and free of dust and grime.

Below are some safe, suggested crystal cleaning methods that range from the simple to the spiritual.

Water Cleansing

Water cleanses are said to not only remove negative energy but also to re-energize a crystal's inherent power.

Crystals can be submerged in fresh distilled water in a non-metallic bowl for up to 2–3 hours. You can also insert your stones in a mesh bag and place in a natural occurring water source, such as a stream, river, or lake.

Another quick and easy way to water cleanse stones is by simply rinsing crystals under cool running faucet water.

Please note: Not all stones react well with water. Research your stones before soaking to be sure water will not have an adverse effect. Avoid water if you are cleansing stones that are particularly porous or have a high metal content.

Salt Water Cleansing

Cleansing stones in salt water can be an effective method, both physically and energetically.

Fill a non-metallic bowl (try glass, ceramic, or wood) with a cup of room temperature distilled water and two tablespoons of sea salt and fully submerge your stones.

You can leave your crystals in this salt-water solution from an hour to overnight.

Following a salt-water soak, rinse crystals thoroughly in cool running water in order to wash away any remaining salt.

Please note: Salt water cleansing can be extremely damaging to some stones. Research your stones before immersing in salt water to be certain they will not be harmed by this method of cleansing. Some stones will break down or deteriorate in salt water. Salt water cleanses are NOT recommended for crystals that contain metal or water or are particularly porous, for example, Pyrite, Lapis Lazuli, Hematite, etc.

Dry Salt Cleansing

Cleansing crystals by submerging them in dry salt is believed to remove negative energies from most stones. Fill a non-metallic bowl with sea salt and bury crystals beneath the salt. Stones can be left in salt for several hours or overnight. Remove crystals and rinse under cool water to remove excess salt. Salt should be disposed of and not re-used.

Please note: Before using any salt-based crystal cleanse, research stones to be certain that salt will not interact negatively with the stones' composition. Dry salt cleanses are NOT recommended for crystals that contain metal or water or are particularly porous, for example, Pyrite, Lapis Lazuli, Hematite, etc.

Smudge Cleansing

Many healers that work with crystals on a regular basis recommend cleansing stones with traditional smudging methods. This simply means burning aromatic smudge sticks or incense and gently fanning the resulting smoke over your stones.

Smudges can be in the form of pre-made incense or dried herbs, plants, and woods. Cedarwood, sage, sweetgrass, and sandalwood are particularly powerful when utilized in this traditional method of crystal cleansing.

Sun and Moon Cleansing

Many crystal healers recommend the natural power of the moon and sun to both cleanse and re-energize and re-charge crystals. This is a beautiful ritual and a wonderful reason to bring your crystals outside and into the natural world. This method is often suggested when first acquiring new stones or cleansing stones that have been frequently handled.

Stones are placed directly outside on grass or soil, or gathered into a non-metallic vessel and left out for a day in the sun or through the night under the moon. Some believe that Full or New Moons can be particularly powerful times to both re-charge and cleanse your stones under moonlight.

When cleaning crystals by the sun, it is best to leave crystals out for no more than an hour and preferably at either sunrise or sunset. Many crystals will fade in color if exposed to strong sunlight for a prolonged period.

STORING CRYSTALS

Many crystals are delicate and certain stones are particularly fragile. Always treat your stones gently.

Where you decide to keep your crystals is a very personal choice, so use your instincts and intuition when choosing where to ultimately place them. One thing to keep in mind is to store "action" stones (crystals that inspire energy or vitality) at a bit of a distance from where you sleep or meditate.

Never hesitate to move your stones, if so inspired. You can try creating your own altar or meditation space. Or simply place crystals among plants or other stones. Or, if you prefer, store them in a soft pouch or keepsake box.

If you decide to put your collection on display, be sure to protect it from direct sun, as the color of some stones may fade with prolonged exposure to bright light. If you prefer to store your stones when not enjoying them, try wrapping crystals in a strong but soft material, such as cotton, silk, velvet, or satin.

MEDITATING WITH CRYSTALS

Crystals are beautiful natural objects or powerful totems, depending on your beliefs. There is no doubt, however, that crystals can enhance meditative states and are effective in signifying and focusing on specific intentions.

When meditating with a crystal, begin by choosing a stone whose meaning feels particularly poignant to you. Select a crystal that resonates instinctually with your present situation and emotional and mental state.

If it is helpful, you can use this guide and read each stone's meaning aloud.

Meditating with your crystal can be as simple as gazing at your stone, holding it in your hand, or simply sitting in a space where it is in close proximity.

You do not have to be in lotus position, nor have your eyes closed. Instead find a posture and a position that is comfortable and calming.

Relax. Breathe.

Focus on your body, the rise and fall of your chest, the expansion of your lungs. Then, focus your attention on the stone, its meaning and your own intent.

Imagine a flow of energy moving up your spine and out of the top of your head.

Relax. Breathe.

Do you want to relax? Do you hope to gain confidence or release fear? Are you seeking resolution or clarity regarding an important decision?

Crystals are a powerful way of tuning in to inner guidance, finding answers to questions we ask of ourselves.

Crystal meditation, like all meditation, is simply a method of anchoring us deeper into our own consciousness.

I   Assists in clarity of communications
II   Promotes self-confidence
III   Encourages articulate self-expression
IV   Supports focused self-transformation
V   Nurtures speaking from the heart
VI   Calms and centers the mind
VII   Relaxes and soothes

BLUE LACE AGATE

I   Grounding, brings one back into the body
II   Activates the senses
III   Energizes life force
IV   Ignites creativity
V   Helps in overcoming artistic blocks
VI   Opens the flow of inspiration
VII   Supports imaginative manifestation, idea into action
VIII Intensifies emotions
IX   Increases passion and sexual energy

FIRE AGATE

I   Awakens compassion
II   Maintains balance and harmony
III   Allows for clear, calm communication
IV   Encourages the setting of boundaries
V   Helps in resolving conflicts
VI   Nurtures confidence and self-love
VII   Enhances intuition
VIII   Guides the seeking of inner truth and clarity

AMAZONITE

I   Nurtures feelings of warmth and well being
II   Increases vitality
III   Promotes clarity of thought and intellectual ability
IV   Cleanses negative energy
V   Encourages manifestation of goals
VI   Clears negative patterns from the past
VII   Purifies and protects
VIII   Facilitates meditation and inner vision

AMBER

I   Ignites spiritual exploration, connection and
      protection
II   Enhances and protects physical environments
III   Wards off negativity
IV   Aids in giving up unwanted habitual behaviors
V   Helps in identifying root causes of deeply held
      behaviors and patterns
VI   Nurtures calmness and clarity
VII   Facilitates meditative states

AMETHYST

I   Encourages centering and grounding
II   Helps to rid one of emotional baggage
III   Supports stillness and calm
IV   Highlights joy in physical experience
V   Counters negative thoughts
VI   Protects from negative energy
VII   Releases emotional blocks
VIII Nurtures stamina and strength

APACHE TEAR

I   Balances energy
II   Encourages emotional healing
III   Removes emotional blocks
IV   Assists in self-awareness and inner work
V   Facilitates connection to higher consciousness and
       meditative states
VI   Offers renewed energy and confidence
VII   Releases attachment to drama and ego

ARAGONITE

I   Balances energy
II   Fosters perseverance
III   Inspires optimism and confidence
IV   Opens the heart to new experiences
V   Helps one to move through change with equilibrium
VI   Assists in releasing attachments to the past
VII   Encourages forward movement
VIII Renews vitality
IX   Nurtures joy, enthusiasm and optimism

GREEN AVENTURINE

I   Ignites positive transformation
II   Relieves loneliness and feelings of isolation
III   Helps with focus and visualization
IV   Increases energy levels
V   Promotes calmness and order
VI   Nurtures healthy relationships and positive group dynamics
VII Encourages feelings of serenity and oneness

BISMUTH

I   Inspires action
II   Supports calm and focused persistence
III   Allows for mental clarity
IV   Encourages focused energy
V   Stimulates the intellect
VI   Relaxes and soothes the mind
VII   Helps to overcome limitations
VIII   Supports calmness and positivity
IX   Enhances self-confidence and courage
X   Removes blocks and fears from the past

HONEY CALCITE

I   Promotes confidence and positive self–esteem
II   Helps to overcome fears and obstacles
III   Encourages action and follow through
IV   Ignites drive for manifestation of goals
V   Strengthens resolves
VI   Activates life force
VII   Fosters sexual energy
VIII   Encourages creativity
IX   Allows for acceptance of change

CARNELIAN

I	Nurtures calm
II	Restores balance
III	Soothes and centers
IV	Focuses one on the present
V	Encourages clarity of communications
VI	Dispels fear and anger
VII	Encourages the seeking of inner knowledge
VIII	Supports self-exploration

BLUE CHALCEDONY

I   Energizes and empowers female energies
II   Allows for clarity of communication
III   Harmonizes and balances energy in the body
IV   Calms and soothes the mind
V   Releases fears, stress and anxiety
VI   Encourages truthful expression and honest exchange
VII   Opens one to the wisdom within

CHRYSOCOLLA

I   Opens inner perception
II   Increases clarity of thought
III   Enhances creativity
IV   Ignites one's power of manifestation
V   Stimulates creativity and imagination
VI   Helps to overcome adversity
VII   Encourages decisive action
VIII   Clears emotional and mental blocks

NATURAL CITRINE

I   Conducts and boosts energy of other crystals
II   Facilitates mental agility and wit
III   Enhances communication
IV   Encourages directness and clarity of thought
V   Increases vitality and energy
VI   Amplifies thoughts and emotions

COPPER

I   Balances and harmonizes emotions
II   Encourages composure and peaceful interaction
III   Inspires playfulness and lighthearted action
IV   Calms anxiety and overactive mind
V   Inspires thoughtfulness and reflection
VI   Strengthens family bonds
VII   Reawakens sense of humor

DALMATIAN STONE

I Calms the mind
II Encourages meditative states
III Aids in mental clarity and acuity
IV Strengthens affirmations
V Helps with focus and attention
VI Protects and neutralizes negative energy
VII Removes energetic blocks
VIII Encourages clarity in decision-making

DESERT ROSE

I   Enhances mental clarity
II   Clears negative energy
III   Improves decision-making abilities
IV   Encourages coherent and incisive thinking
V   Soothes anxieties and stress
VI   Helps with memorization and retention of ideas and information
VII   Ignites clear and cohesive action
VIII   Balances left and right brain

FLUORITE

I   Enhances one's power of attraction
II   Ignites charisma
III   Activates sense of playfulness and fun
IV   Nurtures artistic talents
V   Increases will power
VI   Encourages creativity and manifestation of creative
       goals
VII   Inspires optimism
VIII   Promotes confidence and courage
IX   Helps to overcome creative blocks
X   Stimulates and invigorates physical body

GARNET

I   Stabilizes and balances
II   Allows for grounding, connection to earth and body
III   Balances opposite energies
IV   Harmonizes thought, soothes anxiety
V   Protects and heals
VI   Strengthens resolve and fortitude
VII   Nurtures courage and fearless action

HEMATITE

I   Calms the mind and body
II   Opens one to insight and intuition
III   Increases awareness and mental clarity
IV   Reduces anxiety and stress
V   Relaxes and helps prepare for sleep or rest
VI   Encourages awareness and emotional expression
VII   Helps to decrease anger and frustration

HOWLITE

I   Harmonizes and balances energies
II   Opens the heart
III   Promotes fertility, abundance and growth
IV   Connects one with the natural world
V   Encourages joyful physicality and athleticism
VI   Allows for objectivity in decision-making
VII   Helps to overcome emotional blocks
VIII Inspires generosity and kindness to others

GREEN JADE

I   Nurtures joy
II   Supports feelings of gratitude
III   Expands awareness
IV   Relieves worry and stress
V   Helps to maintain calm and centeredness
VI   Encourages clear communication
VII   Promotes positive self-expression
VIII   Allows for emotional healing

I   Nurtures joy
II   Supports feelings of gratitude
III   Expands awareness

OCEAN JASPER

I   Facilitates meditation
II   Supports inner exploration
III   Encourages grounding and centeredness
IV   Assists with visualization and lucid dreaming
V   Nurtures emotional connection
VI   Harmonizes and balances emotions
VII   Promotes connection to the earth and nature

PICTURE JASPER

I   Balances and stabilizes emotions
II   Encourages grounding and centeredness
III   Enhances relaxation
IV   Nurtures physical vitality
V   Promotes passion and sensuality
VI   Supports inspiration and creativity

I   Purifies and protects
II   Aids in manifestation of goals
III   Inspires direct and focused energy
IV   Helps to rid one of negative patterns and attachments
V   Clears impurities
VI   Absorbs and neutralizes negative energy
VII   Encourages grounding and calmness
VIII   Opens flow of positive energy
IX   Deepens connection to magical energy

JET

I   Grounds and calms
II   Cleanses and repels negative energy
III Helps with the clearing of obstacles and stagnation
IV   Encourages fresh starts and new beginnings
V   Assists with inner exploration and meditation
VII Enhances intuition
VIII Balances and energizes

BLACK KYANITE

I   Inspires higher awareness
II   Allows one to look clearly within
III   Enhances intuition and instinct
IV   Encourages self-discovery
V   Ignites adventures, both inner and outer exploration
VI   Awakens feelings of interconnectedness
VII   Helps to clearly identify and overcome emotional
       blocks
VIII   Increases one's ability to explore the subconscious

LABRADORITE

I   Promotes clarity and self-honesty
II   Elevates the greater good in oneself
III Enhances awareness and intuition
IV   Inspires clear and truthful communication
V   Ignites exploration and knowledge of oneself
VI   Discourages negative thinking
VII Increases ability to overcome negative habits and
     emotional blocks
VIII Assists in visualization and meditation

LAPIS LAZULI

I   Balances and calms
II   Opens the heart
III   Encourages emotional healing
IV   Supports spiritual seeking and inner exploration
V   Unifies and harmonizes energy
VI   Expands the mind
VII   Supports self-guidance and intuition
VIII Nurtures feminine energy
IX   Connects one to ancient knowledge

LEMURIAN SEED

I   Enhances meditative state
II   Releases anxieties and stress
III   Allows one to face challenges with confidence
IV   Guides one to their emotional center
V   Calms the mind and spirit
VI   Curbs hyperactivity
VII   Nurtures acceptance and non-judgment
VIII   Encourages openness and ability to listen
IX   Brings one into the present

LEPIDOLITE

I   Balances emotions
II   Assists in self-reflection and inner exploration
III   Awakens communication between mind and heart
IV   Activates meditative and transcendental experiences
V   Opens one to inner truths
VI   Allows one to release past grievances
VII   Enhances ability to speak truthfully and express
       feelings freely

MAGNESITE

I   Promotes good fortune
II   Protects from negative energies
III   Enhances positivity
IV   Ignites imagination and manifestation of ideas
V   Assists in emotional balance
VI   Inspires responsible and focused action
VII   Encourages creative problem-solving
VIII Nurtures self confidence
IX   Helps to overcome habitual patterns and self-created
      obstacles

MALACHITE

I   Nurtures the divine feminine
II   Purifies and protects
III   Magnifies intentions
IV   Enhances intuition and instinct
V   Balances and aligns energy
VI   Allows for calm and focused manifestation
VII   Encourages deep meditation
VIII Increases clarity of thought and overall awareness
IX   Connects one with the cycles of the moon

MOONSTONE

I   Protects and nurtures
II   Grounds and roots one into the present
III   Allows one to remain centered and focused
IV   Encourages the acceptance of the darker sides of
      one's nature
V   Removes emotional blocks and patterns
VI   Cleanses negative energies

OBSIDIAN

I   Encourages perseverance and focus
II   Allows one to make the best of negative situations
III   Increases intuition and insight
IV   Enhances awareness of the natural world
V   Dissuades one from negative thinking or victim
      mentality
VI   Inspires new ideas
VII   Clears negative energies

SNOWFLAKE OBSIDIAN

I   Enhances inner awareness and self-knowledge
II   Promotes feelings of gratitude and abundance
III   Protects from negative energy
IV   Fosters happiness and positivity
V   Soothes and calms the mind
VI   Aligns and balances energy
VII   Helps in overcoming blocks and obstacles
VIII   Dispels feelings of doubt

PEACOCK ORE

I   Increases vitality and confidence
II   Enhances will power
III   Aids in overcoming bad habits and negative patterns
IV   Anchors one firmly into body
V   Ignites creativity and imaginative thinking
VI   Encourages commitment, perseverance and ambition
VII   Helps with focus and mental clarity
VIII   Supports manifestation and positive action

PYRITE

I   Facilitates connection to higher self
II   Enhances meditation and self-exploration
III   Promotes inner peace
IV   Assists in calm and focused manifestation of goals
V   Aligns and balances energy
VI   Inspires loving communication
VII   Encourages awareness and appreciation of the
       natural world
VIII   Helps to quell anxieties and stress

ANGEL AURA QUARTZ

I   Enhances overall clarity of thought
II   Calms and soothes the mind
III   Promotes serenity and focus
IV   Encourages personal growth and self-expression
V   Increases awareness and meditative focus
VI   Inspires honest communication
VII   Protects against the negative energy of others

AQUA AURA QUARTZ

I   Heightens overall awareness
II   Encourages clarity of thought and communication
III   Amplifies intentions, desires and emotions
IV   Assists in manifestation of goals
V   Clears emotional blocks and self-created obstacles
VI   Enhances meditation
VII   Cleanses negative energy

CLEAR QUARTZ

I   Activates loving energy
II   Promotes compassion and an open heart
III   Dissolves anger and resentment
IV   Releases emotional stress and tensions
V   Inspires harmonious communication and interactions
VI   Soothes and calms the mind
VII   Assists in the release of negative patterns and habits
VIII   Helps in overcoming self-created obstacles

ROSE QUARTZ

I   Promotes calm and grounded action
II   Encourages practicality and organization
III Assists in mental focus and clarity
IV   Neutralizes negative energy
V   Inspires active engagement with the world
VI   Purifies and protects

SMOKY QUARTZ

I   Promotes self-love
II   Inspires confidence and self-willed action
III   Assists in healing emotional wounds
IV   Deepens meditative states
V   Stimulates creativity and imagination
VI   Helps connect to one's child within
VII   Encourages playfulness
VIII Allows for clarity in self-exploration
IX   Pushes one forward, in both action and thought

RHODOCHROSITE

I   Ignites awareness and inner vision
II   Clears negative energy
III   Dissolves blocks and self-created obstacles
IV   Promotes positive action
V   Encourages manifestation of goals
VI   Aids in overcoming stagnation
VII   Inspires lucid dreaming and visual meditations
VIII Connects to spiritual energy and spiritual cleansing

SELENITE

I   Heightens awareness
II   Attracts positive energy
III   Expands consciousness and inner vision
IV   Empowers and strengthens resolve
V   Deflects negative energy
VI   Enhances intuition
VII   Inspires friendship and kindness to others

TEKTITE

I   Balances energy
II   Increases mental clarity
III   Ignites creativity
IV   Soothes discord within relationships
V   Encourages vitality and strength
VI   Promotes practicality in action
VII   Inspires harmony of opposites
VIII Opens the mind
IX   Allows one to make discerning, nonjudgmental
       decisions

TIGER'S EYE

I	Purifies and protects
II	Encourages calm and rational problem-solving
III	Deflects anger
IV	Clears negatives energies
V	Promotes harmony and balance
VI	Rids one of anxieties and fears
VII	Grounds and calms the mind and body
VIII	Releases one from negative behavior patterns
IX	Helps in overcoming chronic worry and negative habits

BLACK TOURMALINE

INTERVIEWS WITH CONTEMPORARY CRYSTAL ARTISTS & HEALERS

Part of what fueled the manifestation of this book—and the entire New New Age Series—is a deep curiosity about the ways in which we explore and connect with our spirituality in the modern world.

To that end, we spoke with several contemporary artists and healers, those who utilize crystals as primary tools and inspiration in their work. We asked them to discuss what led them to the study of stones, how they integrate that study into their personal and professional lives, and why they feel there has been such a strong resurgence of interest, in the new Millennium, in spirituality, magic, and the cosmos.

We discussed stones with the following: Azalea Lee is a crystal healer who founded Place 8 Healing in Los Angeles. Also the designer of the metaphysical jewelry line As Above So Below, Lee has been a spiritual seeker her whole life, working as a wardrobe stylist and costume designer prior to finding her calling as a crystal healer.

Sherise Lee is a Chinese-American mother, artist, designer and experimenter of the tactile and the incorporeal. Also known as The Radder—a traveling market, online shop and blog—she lives in the Los Angeles area with her two sons, husband and future dog.

Gia Bahm is the creator of the jewelry line Unearthen. She selects ethically sourced stones and metals according to their histories and qualities.

Shannon Ross of Sun Moon Nation has spent the last five years designing jewelry and interiors, always including prayers and crystals. She lives on the Caribbean coast of Costa Rica, teaching the Human Crystal Journey and sharing tools of creative heart alchemy.

Erica Clum is a wardrobe stylist and costumer for film and television, owner of the Los Angeles-based vintage store Goldmine, and founder of jewelry line Earthling. The line is inspired by the sacred geometry of crystals, by rocks and rust and treasures buried deep in the ground.

What first drew you to working with stones?

Azalea Lee: In one way you could say it began as a hobby of rock hounding, which is hand-digging crystals and stones from the ground. My husband and I found a rare benitoite crystal large enough to be cut into a gemstone. I hadn't cared much for gems and didn't even wear my engagement ring, but there was something special about this stone we had found together. So I began searching for someone to cut the gem and was introduced to the work of a custom gemstone cutter by the name of Jean-Noel Soni.

My friend had shown me a stone Jean had cut and it blew my mind. I had never seen before a gemstone so thoughtfully, carefully, and passionately sculpted. I met Jean the next day and intuitively chose some stones for him to cut into my own personalized, metaphysical jewelry. I didn't know the metaphysical properties of the stones I commissioned from him, but somehow I knew those gemstones were right for me and that I would create very personal metaphysically supportive pieces of jewelry for myself.

After making some initial pieces, I then began feeling like I wanted to make supportive jewelry like this for other people. But I didn't want to read from some book that a particular crystal had a certain metaphysical property; because that just felt too much like, "The Bible tells me so." So I decided to take a crystal-healing course to see if I had any affinity for understanding the crystals.

In my first crystal healing class, I had to do a crystal healing for my teacher's friend as my teacher watched so that if I got stuck she could help me. At the end of the session, she said to her friend, "Can you believe this is her first time?" I had just known how to work with the crystals to do the healing. And with that I walked out of my class in a stunned daze. Because since I was a very little girl, I knew I came into this world to do some work. I had been telling the Universe my whole life that I would do whatever it asked me to do. Decades rolled by, and I was deeply frustrated that the Universe was not telling me exactly what my purpose was. But through a series of what I thought were random intuitive directives from the Universe, at 37, I was finally led to my purpose as a crystal healer.

Gia Bahm: I was living in New York and had already been making jewelry for look books and other photo shoots I was doing costumes for, but hadn't started Unearthen yet. My friend from LA came to visit and said she wanted to check out a crystal store in Midtown, so on a humid hot summer day we rode our bikes from Brooklyn to the store and low and behold, it was like the opening of a new world to me. All of my childhood memories of visiting the Natural History Museum, my rock polishing kit, and combing the beach for treasures were all re-sparked and I was just instantly obsessed and mystified. I had always thought that crystals were somehow unobtainable in the forms I would want since being a little kid, but after visiting this store, the whole thing just kind of exploded for me.

Sherise Lee: Jade has a history in China of at least four thousand years. Jade symbolizes many things that the Chinese admire: honor, conviction, love for others and the stone itself is a literal expression of beauty, is considered to be "the essence of heaven and earth," with healing quali-ties for the physical body. This was just a fact growing up Chinese-American.

Along with that, I, like many who study crystal healing, have been collecting stones since I was a kid. In elementary school, I had jars full of rocks and divided them by color. In high school, I practiced Tarot and wore jewelry with sacred stones but didn't yet understand their properties. Most recently, after being introduced by Agnes Badoo and Wendy Polish to Azalea Lee of Place 8 Healing and having an incredibly transformational crystal healing from her, I had to learn more.

Shannon Ross: My intrigue with crystals began while living on an island in Tofino, a surf town on Vancouver Island in Canada. An old boyfriend had given me a clear quartz crystal in the Black Rock desert the summer before.

One night alone on the 50-acre island, while my island partner was in Vancouver for work, I found the crystal among my craft supplies. I brought it with me to the bedroom for a meditation. I built a little fire in the fireplace, lit some candles at my altar, burned some incense and opened the doors onto the pond for some nature nighttime sounds.

All I had been doing that week was yoga, surfing, hiking, hula hooping, canoeing, and building and planting multiple herb and vegetable gardens on the property, one in the shape of a crescent moon, mirroring the one in the sky. Needless to say I was very in-tune with myself and the earth.

I find, in silence paired with nature, questions—big philosophical questions—begin to rise. So, while in deep meditation that night, it dawned on me to ask these questions to the crystal. What I found was that it had answers.

A little over a year later, in October 2011, I started a crystal jewelry line guided by an encounter with a crystal shop, the Eye of Horus, and a falcon. Every necklace I made was a prayer of peace, creativity, and abundance. Each one was unique, and each one I made sold like magic. I have been interacting with crystals on the daily and looking into their rainbow reflections ever since.

Erica Clum: I started collecting rocks when I was a kid. I would walk for hours looking down at the ground searching for treasures. There were a lot of arrowheads where I grew up made out of flint. I was fascinated by them. When I discovered the fancier rocks, crystal points and Herkimer diamonds (they are mined in the town my Grandma was born in), I was amazed that these things grew that way and were hidden beneath the ground, often inside another not as pretty rock once you cracked it open. It was pure magic. They've been around my whole life. The reason I started making jewelry was so the stones didn't have to just stay home on a shelf.

Can you speak a bit to your method of study?

AL: The kind of crystal healing I do involves assessing the energy of a person and then placing a unique combination of crystals on and around their body. The combined energy of crystals trigger an inner journey which is deeply visual, auditory, and visceral. It is through this journey where I can help my clients uncover a deeper understanding of why they are going through events in their life and what they truly need to heal. The thing I hear most often people say as a result of their sessions is that it brings them a deep clarity about their lives.

These inner journeys instigated by the crystals can include experiences of color and texture, seemingly random childhood memories, past lives, meetings with spirit animals or guides, or even just abstract shapes which can be entered and experienced. With every crystal healing session I never know where we are going to go. But I know whatever is needed most for healing for the client will come up. But every single session is like entering someone's energetic movie.

My job is to hold the space of healing and help any unbalanced energies follow the balanced vibrational energies of the crystals by selectively choosing the most helpful crystals for that person's healing. This may involve up to a hundred crystals being strategically placed in a grid on the body to help with this alignment. One way I can describe the experience for me is feeling like a chiropractor, except I'm adjusting energy. But really, it's always the client that is actually directing and engaging their own healing.

I personally studied under Katrina Raphaell who is one of the godmothers of crystal healing. She has a trilogy of crystal healing books that have been continually in print for the last thirty years.

Her teachings gave me the framework for understanding the methods of doing crystal healing, as well as the introductory knowledge of stones. But since I have turned on my receptivity to the stones, my understanding of the metaphysical properties comes from being able to personally communicate with the stones, as well as seeing the reoccurring results from intuitively working with clients.

SL: I approach studying stones and crystals as I do every topic I deeply want to learn, by learning the foundation from as close to the source as possible. Through Azalea Lee, I was introduced to Krystal Eri who Azalea learned from and who was also a long-time student of Katrina Raphaell. From there, I went on to learn from Naisha Ahsian. Every day for several months, I devoted hours to deep meditation, listening to stones and studying them. My goal was to be in complete vibration with that particular stone and element (earth, fire, storm, etc.), to understand it fully and not impress any of my preconceived notions onto it. It is also important for me to learn from different schools of thought, absorb that and create my own form. I am still a student, and will always be.

Naisha Ahsian has been a true mentor and teacher, and Katrina Raphaell through her books and learning within her school. And Azalea is always spot on when picking a stone for you.

GB: The first book I got about crystals is called *Love is in the Earth*, the author's name is Melody (with a music note after it). Pretty amazing. That's the one I have found to be the most in depth, and there are several editions after the original book with more stone types and updated information.

When I started Unearthen in 2007, I created with a writing partner our own meanings of stones, which you can find on our Unearthen web site under "Stone Properties." We are always updating it and adding more.

SR: My method of study is to use gemstones to connect with mama earth and her soft wisdom. I study the crystals themselves, online research, their colors as a chakra vibration. I also love the book *Love is in the Earth* by Melody.

EC: I like the book *Love is in the Earth* by Melody and Judy Hall's *The Crystal Bible*. My friends Mark and Martin at Spellbound Sky and also my pal Rachel—she's an encyclopedia of stones. I will shoot her a text asking what stone will give me whatever property I am looking for or a picture of a stone I can't quite place. She's a real gem.

How do you select stones for yourself?

AL: Because my intuition is now deeply connected with the mineral kingdom, I select stones intuitively for myself. This may come from being suddenly attracted to a stone aesthetically, but I'm strongly clairvoyant so I just know when a stone is right for me. And sometimes the crystals will literally shout at me when they want me to pay attention them.

GB: I make pieces for the main collection based on what I think is beautiful and interesting at the moment. I make a lot of custom work as well, and those tend to focus in the beginning more on the stones meanings, which I also love.

SL: I practice crystal tarot. From there a stone will reveal itself and then I work with it for about a week. When I am out and about, I intuitively seek stones first by visual appearances, then holding and feeling their messages in my receptive (left) hand.

SR: I follow divine guidance, feeling into the energy of the stones, and if they are for other people, the energy field of that person.

EC: Stone selection for me is mostly aesthetic. I am very visual and I look for the ones that draw me in. The energetic properties, I am sure have something to do with it, though on a more subconscious level.

Gia and Erica, what are the primary inspirations for your jewelry?

GB: You might not guess this, but music has a lot to do with my inspiration. It allows me to focus and interpret the visual when I have auditory stimulation. It helps me to create a physical form from a thought in my brain. It kind of creates the whole world, if that makes sense. Nature and the insurmountable power and beauty it holds. Botany, architecture, perfume, and other designers who take their art one step further.

EC: My jewelry is mostly inspired by what the stone wants. I choose them first and then spend a little time with them to see how they'd best like to be mounted into a piece of jewelry. My inspiration for becoming a jeweler was to create pieces that focused on the stone and I wanted them to look as close to the way they came out of the earth as possible on your finger. I have since branched out in my designs to incorporate symbols, talismans, mythology (some of which I make up).

Do you have particular stones you feel powerfully drawn to?

AL: Yes, personally I am strongly attuned to phenakite. But there are stones like hematite and black tourmaline that may not have as intense of a vibration as stones like phenakite, but are deeply important and trusted supporters of my energy.

GB: Yes, so many! I love opals for their lightness and incredible natural rainbow, jaspers for their intricateness and strong aesthetic, clear quartz for its versatile and chic feel, geodes because they are like looking into tiny worlds. I could go on. These stones also all obviously have their own properties and health benefits, but on the surface for making jewelry, it's sometimes what I think of first when designing.

SL: All forms of quartz! The second most abundant mineral in the Earth's continental crust. It holds so much knowledge and history. It is abundant for a reason. Work with what is there. It's okay for things to be easy. Why hold high that which is difficult? I digress.

When I first began, I was drawn to and worked with a small, beautiful piece of azurite, but it was too strong for me as a beginner and just blew my top open. I wasn't ready and therefore closed myself for about a year, before grounding myself and truly learning how to work with stones. Currently, I am really coveting a big hunk of love from Himalayan quartz.

SR: My most loved crystals are quartz crystals because they are the strongest and clearest energy portals. Rainbow moonstone is my other favorite to enhance my connection to my intuition and dreams. Selenite is also a favorite in connecting with my higher self, my most fully expressed self.

EC: Yes! The Herkimer diamonds, which are double terminated quartz, not actual diamonds. The one place in the world where they are found is in the town my Grandmother was born in so they are very special to me. I also have strong feelings for labradorite, moonstone, and turquoise.

Why do you think there has been such a resurgence lately in our fascination with stones?

AL: In Atlantian and Lemurian times, crystals were used as a major form of technology, but this technology became abused for ill cause. The information was lost with the end of these civilizations except for a few bits of information carried with those who survived those environmental catastrophes. The current crystal resurgence is happening because we are entering an era of major energetic shifts and there are many of us that are finally now spiritually evolved enough to use crystalline power again in a beneficial way for the world so that we can heal it and ourselves.

GB: I think everyone is emotionally motivated about the things they choose to spend their time, money, and energy on. If there is a way to create more meaning, then we are all for it. Crystals support that cause—whether you choose to believe it or just use it as a keepsake to remind yourself of the goals you are trying to achieve, it's all for the betterment of one's self, and society as a whole.

SL: I think it will take several more generations before crystals are just a part of regular life in the Western world. In the U.S., we have seen older generations swing through the opening of consciousness and only begin to realize what other cultures have known since the beginning to be true through validation, science, and human exploration. They'll figure it out at some point. Hopefully before the earth is destroyed. I remain positive and believe in humanity though.

SR: People are waking up to the fact that all life is a dance of energy on a crystal ball we call earth. Crystals hold and move energy within our fields and our lives. Paired with the power of intention and ritual, anything is possible.

Our culture is finally finding freedom beyond linear reality. Life is a spiral journey from inside to outside. Everything that has ever been created is from our imaginations. The words, stories, and belief systems we adhere to make up our lives. What do you want to believe in, what do you want to create?

May we all choose thoughts, words, and actions that support our health and happiness, and the health and happiness of each other, and the earth.

EC: I think we are evolving as a people, that we are on the cusp of entering into a new age. People are becoming more sensitive, and veils are being lifted. Genders are blurred. Science and spirituality are coming together. People are looking for truth.

Biographies

Jessica Hundley is the founder of The Good Word Creative Agency. She is an author and editor of several books on music, art, film, and design. She has been fascinated, since childhood, by plants, stones, crystals, and the inherent magic of the natural world.

A California native, **Paul N. Collins** moved east and honed his photo skills in New York City for over a decade. Now back on the West Coast, Paul spends his time getting lost on BLM land, National Forests, and the Pacific Ocean. He firmly believes that "reality is stranger than fiction" and loves telling stories via photography of the orphans, brawlers, and bastards that he meets in his ramblings. His work has been featured in *Hemispheres*, *Stay Wild*, *Desert Magazine*, *Indoek*, *The Adventure Handbook* and more.

Acknowledgments

Much gratitude goes to all who helped manifest this book: George Augusto, J.C. Gabel, Brian Roettinger, Taylor Giali, Lisa Bechtold, Mark Phillips, Martin Anguiano, and Paul N. Collins.

In addition to our work with Spellbound Sky, we spent time speaking with and researching work from a variety of modern crystal healers, and those that paved the way before them. All the content included in this book was double-checked, cross-referenced and inspired by the good work of the following healers, educators and experts. We encourage you to delve into their websites, social media feeds and publications for deeper insight into crystals and their inherent powers.

Thank you: Robert Simmons and Naisha Ahsian, authors of *The Book of Stones* / Judy Hall, author of *The Crystal Bible* and *Encyclopedia of Crystals* / Katrina Raphaell, founder of The Crystal Academy of Advanced Healing Arts in Taos, New Mexico, and author of *Crystal Enlightenment*, *Crystal Healing*, *Crystalline Transmission* and *Crystalline Illumination* / Melody, author of *Love is in the Earth* / Shannon Ross of Sun Moon Nation / Azalea Lee of Place 8 Healing and As Above, So Below / Jessica Snow Meditation / Anja of Woodlights Woudlicht / Erica Clum of Earthling Jewelry / Gia Bahm of Unearthen / The Crystal Matrix / House of Intuition / Arlene Uribe of Sacred Light / Goldirocks / Luminosity Crystals.

The New New Age Series: Crystals

First North American Edition 2017

Copyright © 2017 by Hat & Beard Press,
Los Angeles

Copyright © 2017 by Dilettante Paper,
Los Angeles

Except for select photographs and
images authorized for press and
promotion, no part of this book may be
reproduced in any form by any means,
electronic or mechanical, including
photocopying and recording, or by any
information storage and retrieval system,
without permission in writing from the
publishers.

ISBN: 978-0-9987239-2-1

Editor: Jessica Hundley
Design: Taylor Giali
Photography: Paul N. Collins

Hat & Beard Press books are printed by
The Avery Group at Shapco Printing in
Minneapolis, Minnesota.

Hat & Beard Press
1726 North Spring Street
Los Angeles, California 90012

Dilettante Paper
120 North Sante Fe Avenue
Los Angeles, California 90012

www.hatandbeard.com
www.dilpaper.com